Journaling the Chakras

Eight Weeks to Self-Discovery

Amber Lea Starfire

MoonSkye Publishing

NAPA, CA

MoonSkye Publishing
1351 2nd Street, #5562
Napa, CA 94581

Book Layout © 2017 BookDesignTemplates.com
Cover Design by Amber Lea Starfire

Journaling the Chakras/ Amber Lea Starfire — 1st ed.
ISBN 978-0-9848636-8-6

What you seek is seeking you.

— Jalaluddin Rumi —

Contents

Introduction

Welcome to a unique spiritual writing adventure —
a journey of self-discovery and personal growth. Using the techniques and prompts provided in these
pages, you will wind your way through the real and
metaphorical chakras of your life, beginning with
the root chakra (related to instinct, security, survival, and human potential) and ending with the crown
chakra (related to consciousness and connection
with the divine). In the process, you will reveal the
various ways you experience your life. Employing
journal writing to reflect on different aspects of your
inner self — and how you express or experience it —
can both enlighten and heal.

Journaling, when we give ourselves to it, engages all
aspects of our being — body, mind, heart, and soul
— and is therefore a unique tool for self-discovery
and creative expression.

I originally designed *Journaling the Chakras* as an eight-week course to experience and share in a small group. I believe that when we take part with others in visualization and journal writing exercises we enrich and inform one another. However, there are also benefits to studying on one's own, and it's unnecessary to be in a group to learn and grow. So, whether you go through this journey with others or by yourself, I invite you to dedicate time each day to reading the information and performing the exercises in this book. I guarantee you will discover and bring to light things about yourself of which you were previously unaware.

Journaling the Chakras is not about criticizing your writing skills, grammar, or spelling. It is not about judging yourself or fretting about whether you and your writing are "good enough."

In *Journaling the Chakras*, I provide guidance and techniques to help you create a safe space in which to inquire, write, explore, reflect, read, receive intuitive feedback, learn, write more, and develop the habit of daily journal writing. It is my desire and hope that as you travel this journey of spiritual and emotional self-discovery, you will write your way to wholeness.

How to Use this Book

For best results, work your way through the book from beginning to end. I've arranged the chapters in the same order as the Chakras, Root Chakra to Crown and ending with a chapter on integrating what you've learned and experienced into a whole and balanced energy system.

Recommended pace:

Week 1   Day 1: Read Chapter One — Begin at the Beginning, including the Introduction to Meditation and Pre-writing instructions.

Days 2-7: Read and do the meditations and writing exercises in Chapter Two — Planting the Soul.

Week 2   Read and do the meditations and writing exercises in Chapter Three — Going with the Flow.

Week 3   Read and do the meditations and writing exercises in Chapter Four — Taking Action

Week 4   Read and do the meditations and writing exercises in Chapter Five — Balancing Mind, Body, and Heart

Week 5   Read and do the meditations and writing exercises in Chapter Six — Speaking Out

Week 6   Read and do the meditations and writing exercises in Chapter Seven — Receiving Inspiration

Week 7   Read and do the meditations and writing exercises in Chapter Eight — Mind and Spirit

Week 8   Read and do the meditations and writing exercises in Chapter Nine — Integration.

Though you may, of course, take as long as you want to focus on the exercises and writing prompts in each chapter, I encourage to explore each chakra at a pace no faster than one chakra per week, as outlined above.

Chapter One

Begin at the Beginning

An Overview of the Seven Chakras

The word "chakra" is a Sanskrit word that means "wheel" or "disc." According to Indian traditions, the chakras are wheel-like centers of energy. Though there are many chakras throughout the body, we each have seven major chakras, located along the line of energy following the spinal column. Chakras are not visible to the naked eye, but exist as part of the invisible being, or "etheric double" of human beings.

Each of these chakras takes in and expresses vital life force energy, and each chakra corresponds with different aspects of our physical, mental/emotional and spiritual beings.

One way of describing the functions of the chakras is that they are portals that transfer or translate energy from one plane (or level of existence) to the next — spirit to matter and vice versa. The chakras are in the physical body, yet they are not physical. You can visualize them as the place where spirit and body join or meet.

When the chakras are open and in balance, our life force flows freely through our body. We are healthy and operating at peak energetic capacity. When chakras are out of balance, not functioning properly, or when the flow of energy is blocked, physical or mental/emotional illness can result. An open energy flow is our natural state of being, and a blocked energy flow a result of our responses to difficult life experiences.

Each chakra corresponds to a color, a particular area of the body, an element (earth, air, fire, water), and a sound.

There are different branches of ancient traditions and new-age religions which have developed various adaptations of and names for the chakra system, but they all have the same theoretical base.

The lower three chakras relate to our physical life, the upper three chakras relate to our spiritual life, and the fourth chakra — central to our body and our energetic system — balances the physical and spiritual aspects of our being.

First, or Root Chakra

The Root Chakra is at the base of the spine, at the tailbone. This chakra is the center of physical energy and vitality. It corresponds with issues of self-preservation, the will to live, security, safety, and primal erotic and procreational instincts. The Root relates to how we take care of ourselves. Physically, the root chakra governs the adrenals, spinal column, kidneys, colon, legs, and bones. The color of the root chakra is red and the chant associated with it is LAM.

Second, or Sacral Chakra

The Sacral Chakra is at the sacrum (giving it its name). Key issues of the sacral chakra include relationships, pleasure, sensuality, sexuality, intuition, expression of emotions, and basic emotional needs. It is also the sexual center for women. The sacral chakra governs the skin, spleen, lower back and reproductive system. The color of the sacral chakra is orange and the chant is VAM.

Third, or Solar Plexus Chakra

The Solar Plexus Chakra lives where its name suggests. This chakra is the center of your personal power. Key issues of the solar plexus chakra include power, fear, anxiety, introversion/extroversion, personal growth, and expansion. The solar plexus chakra governs digestion, the nervous system, pancreas, gall bladder, and liver. The color of the solar plexus chakra is yellow and the chant is RAM.

Fourth, or Heart Chakra

The Heart Chakra is in the center of the body in the heart region. It is the bridge between the earthly chakras below, and the spiritual chakras above. It is the center of love, compassion, and human potential. The heart chakra governs the heart, blood, and circulatory system. The color of the heart chakra is green and the chant is YAM.

Fifth, or throat Chakra

The throat chakra resides at the base of the throat, at the dimple between the two collarbones. This chakra is the center of communication, of "speaking your truth." Key issues of the throat chakra include the ability to speak up, communication, expression of thoughts and creativity, and being true to self. The throat chakra governs the bronchial and vocal apparatus and the lungs. The color of the throat chakra is blue and the chant is HAM.

Sixth, or Third-Eye Chakra

The Third-Eye Chakra, also sometimes referred to as the brow chakra is in the center of the forehead on the front of the body and at the base of the skull at the back. This chakra is the center of intuition, wisdom, and psychic powers. The third-eye chakra governs the lower brain, left eye, ears, nose, and nervous system. The color of the head chakra is indigo (a kind of dark purple) and the chant is OM (or AUM).

Seventh, or Crown Chakra

The Crown Chakra is at the top of the head. This chakra is the center of connection to universal energy, or the divine. Key issues of the crown chakra include connection to divinity, Truth, and spiritual knowledge. The crown chakra governs the upper brain and right eye. The colors associated with the crown chakra are violet, white, and sometimes gold, and the chant is NG.

Introduction to Prewriting, Meditation, & Visualization Techniques

Each day, before journaling, take between five and twenty minutes, depending upon your time and inclinations, to engage in prewriting meditation and visualization techniques.

These activities will calm you, bring you to an introspective or "inner" state of mindfulness, and help you focus on and raise awareness of the particular chakra we are working with during that lesson.

Meditations can take the form of walking, touching, breathing mindfulness, and/or deep relaxation.

As an introductory exercise, and to prepare for the upcoming lessons, practice the following 10-minute exercise:

1. Sit in a chair with your back straight or lie in a comfortable position on the floor, whichever you prefer. Close your eyes and focus on your breath as it flows in and out of your body. You need not

change how you are breathing. Follow the flow of air as it enters and leaves your body. You may find it helpful to repeat words in your mind, such as "following the breath in, following the breath out," as you do this.

2. When you feel calm and focused, imagine a golden tube of light extending the length of your spine, from your tailbone to your crown. Now imagine a ball of golden-white light floating above your head. As you breathe in, the ball of light sinks gently from the crown to the center of your body, to the heart region. As you breathe out, imagine the glow of the ball expanding outward and filling your body with light. Continue breathing, following your breath, imagining the light continuing to grow until it expands beyond your body and fills the room with light.

3. Play with this, letting the light expand and contract with your breath, noticing how you feel.

4. When you are ready, imagine the light contracting until it fits comfortably within your body,

allow the ball to return gently to the top of your head, and open your eyes.

5. Write for five minutes about your experience. Do not let your pen leave the paper (or your fingers the keyboard if you are using a computer); keep writing for at least five minutes.

Chapter Two

Planting the Soul
The Root Chakra

Muladhara

Element: Earth
Color: Red
Sound: LAM

The root chakra is our energetic foundation. At the base of the spine, between the coccyx and the pelvic bone, the chakra draws energy upward and into our bodies from the Earth.

The root chakra is all about being in our bodies, providing a foundation for our journey through life in the vehicle of the physical body. This chakra literally grounds our soul in the physical, and the strength of the root chakra corresponds with our strength of will and desire to live. The first chakra helps us learn how to control and coordinate our movements in the physical world. It is our beginning and our link to the Earth, our foundation. And because it is about drawing energy in, it is also the center of our ability to manifest.

This red chakra, represented by the element of earth, reminds us of our individual uniqueness and identity. It provides us with focus, discipline, and an anchor from which to grow.

We begin our long journey upward through the chakras with our first chakra, the base of our body, our past, and the unconscious. This is a primal place, connecting us to the Earth through our instincts — both programmed physical responses (breath and the beating of our hearts) and the instinct of self-preservation. We don't think about these things; they just happen.

Many of us have been taught that to be spiritually enlightened we have to transcend our bodies, with their physical desires and pleasures. However, pulling a plant out of the ground won't help it grow, and it's the same with us. We need our roots to be fully developed and connected to the Earth to grow upwards. And in this journey through the chakras, we need to go down into the core of our body, into our past, and into the developmental phase of our root chakra, which is the first year of life.

When we come into this world, we are helpless, unknowing, a bundle of raw energy. We have just emerged from the quiet predictability of the womb to the chaos of the world with its noise and light. How might we feel at that moment of birth?

If we are immediately loved and welcomed, and if our physical needs for warmth, comfort, and food are met, we relax into a sense of safety. Being in the body becomes a comfortable experience, and we develop a sense of trust. If we are not loved and welcomed, we may learn to fear this new environment. That fear lodges in the root chakra, and we develop a sense of mistrust, perhaps feeling an inability to meet the demands of survival.

During our first year of life, our task is to learn how to operate our bodies: regulate body temperature, digest food, and orient ourselves in the physical environment. All of this becomes our realm of experience, which underlies and creates a foundation for our future. If we're given support to learn, we develop a sense of power and confidence. We develop a sense of the right to be here on Earth.

If we don't develop those strong roots, we may struggle our entire lives with an underlying sense of insecurity and inadequacy, feeling we don't belong in this world.

When the root chakra is balanced and energy flows freely through it, we enjoy good physical health, safety, security, a sense of enjoyment and stability in life. We know we can make things work to survive, and we enjoy a sense of prosperity.

All of that sounds simple, but energy in any of our chakras can become imbalanced or blocked due to our early and developmental responses to events and stimuli we experience.

For example, injuries or imbalances can occur to the root chakra through early traumas: a child is born with the chord wrapped around his neck, preventing him from breathing right away; a premature infant is taken away from her mother and placed in an incubator, preventing that important, immediate bonding with her mother; another child's physical needs for food and shelter aren't met; a child is abandoned or given to someone else to raise; and someone else experiences physical abuse.

In response to these early traumas, a child might withdraw, contract, and try to stop the flow of energies barraging her. That child may develop a sense of not belonging, constant loneliness, a desire to escape life through drugs or suicide, or a persistent sense of disappointment and/or ambivalence about life.

Health of Your Root Chakra

So how do you know if your chakra is open and spinning the way it should be? We will use pre-writing visualization and journaling with writing prompts to determine the current state of our chakras and to promote health and healing.

You will need a minimum of 20 minutes for both activities. Be sure to arrange a time and place where you can work undisturbed.

Pre-Writing Visualization

Before responding to the following writing prompts, perform the this 10-minute visualization exercise. Read the instructions through before starting. This exercise also works well any time you feel a need to ground yourself.

Root Chakra Visualization Activity

Sit or stand in a comfortable position. For the root chakra, I like to stand, because I can feel energy moving straight through my body, but sitting in a comfortable position will work. Be sure that your feet are flat on the floor.

Close your eyes and, for two or three slow breaths, follow your breath in and out of your body, feeling your lungs expand and fill with each intake and contract and empty with each outflow. Allow a natural pause at the end of each inhale and exhale. As you breathe out, allow your body to relax. Let your cares and thoughts flow out of your body with each exhale.

On the next breath, send a golden root from the area between your legs, from your perineum, the base of your root chakra, deep into the Earth. Visualize it spreading out, like the roots of a tree. When you are ready, send two more golden roots through the soles of your feet into the Earth. Stay with this for a few breaths, sending the roots deeper with each breath.

When you are ready, breathe in and imagine that you are drawing energy as golden light up through your roots from the Earth, up through your legs and into the area at the base of your spine. Imagine the energy pausing and hovering there as a ball of red light. Feel the strength of your connection to the Earth, your feet planted.

Each time you exhale, imagine the red ball of light glowing and expanding slightly. Each time you inhale, imagine drawing more energy upward from the Earth. into the ball of light

Repeat this visualization of breathing energy into your root chakra for at least two minutes. Let the red glow expand to fill your hips, your legs and your feet.

While you do this, notice how the light looks and feels in your imagination. Can you visualize the glowing ball, or is it something that you feel more than see? Is it a bright red or a deep red? Transparent or obscure? Round or oblong or another shape? Is it spinning or moving? If so, in which direction? Can you feel its energy? Is it warm or cold? Don't make judgments about what it "should" or "should not" be looking like or doing. Just notice what you notice.

Now, send love to the area of your root chakra. Notice if the light changes. Keep sending love while continuing to imagine the energy flowing from the Earth and into the red light. Stay here as long as you feel comfortable and have time.

When you are ready, let the flow of energy subside, and the red ball of light contract until it is centered again between your legs, above the perineum, in your lower pelvic area. Allow your roots to gently withdraw from the Earth, back into your body.

Open your eyes.

Writing Prompts

Choose one of the following prompts. Then, write for ten minutes in response to the prompt. Let your thoughts and feelings flow. If a particular incident or memory comes up, write about it. Get as much onto the page in ten minutes as you can.

When the ten minutes is up, stop, close your eyes and breathe, counting five long breaths. While you are breathing, imagine your root chakra as a ball of red light at the base of your spine. How does it feel? Open your eyes. If you want to write more, go ahead.

1. Write anything about your root chakra visualization that comes to mind: feelings, thoughts, or pictures (yes, I encourage you to draw!).

2. How do you feel about life? Do you think life is hard or easy? Are you excited about the future or concerned about bad things that might happen? Do you identify yourself as optimistic or pessimistic? Which of your life events have confirmed your sense of optimism or pessimism?

3. Think back to when you were young. What are your earliest memories? Bring yourself back to that time when you were a child and write about how you feel. Do you feel loved and safe, or insecure? Do you feel comfortable being you, or do you hide yourself from others to be safe?

4. What do you do that feels nurturing and comforting to you? Write five activities you like to do to calm and comfort yourself during times of stress or crisis. When did you start doing these activities? What events occurred around that same time in your life?

5. How do you feel about your body? Do you love it? Does it feel good? Or is it something you drag around with you? How did you feel about your body when you were a child? Do you feel different now? What events shaped your view and feelings about your body?

6. How do you nourish yourself physically? Does your food give you what you need, help you to be healthy and maintain a balanced weight? How

do you feel about food? If food were a person, how would you describe your relationship with it?

7. How do you nourish yourself emotionally? Do you engage in activities that comfort and help you to feel safe and nurtured? If so, what do you do? What about those activities nurtures you? If you don't nourish yourself emotionally, or feel it's not enough, what prevents you from doing more? What excuses or reasons do you give yourself for not nourishing yourself emotionally?

8. How do you feel about your place on this earth? Do you believe you are here for a purpose? Do you feel you belong? Or do you wonder if there is any meaning to life? Do you search for a sense of belonging that seems to evade you? What events, influences, and people have shaped your sense of belonging and purpose?

9. How do you express yourself in the world? How do you earn your living? Do you like it? How does your work feel in your body?

Chapter Three

Going with the Flow
The Sacral Chakra

Swadhisthana

Element: *Water*
Color: *Orange*
Sound: *VAM*

The sacral chakra is the center of emotion and physical pleasure. Located just above the root chakra, in the lower abdominal (sacral) area, this chakra moves our energy to the next level, from the element earth (solid, slow, quiet) to the element water (movement, flowing, liquid). The sacral chakra is the seat of sexual, erotic energy, but this is not its only function. It also corresponds to creativity, joy, manifestation, relationships, and personal power. The sacral chakra rules the sexual organs, urinary tract, lower intestines, spinal fluid, low back, and the largest sensual organ, the skin.

When this chakra is open and functioning, you allow yourself to experience your feelings fully, while not dwelling on them. You are comfortable with your sexuality and enjoy strong and healthy (not addictive) sexual energy. In addition, you experience joy in life, the ability to let go of things you cannot control, and have healing energy. You allow yourself to enjoy abundance and to receive the things you desire.

When the sacral chakra is blocked or not functioning properly, possible issues include guilt, low sex drive, reproductive problems, control and power issues, addictions to drugs or alcohol, trouble handling money, difficulty in your relationships, and strong emotional swings or moodiness. You may be over-sensitive, repress emotions, and/or deal with depression. You may repress desires and not allow yourself to receive love and/or financial abundance.

Physical issues related to this chakra include low back pain, sciatica, problems with the sexual organs, sex drive, and urinary tract problems.

Developmentally, this chakra comes into play when we are approximately six months' old. It moves us to a place of duality: pleasure vs. pain, good vs. bad, and give vs. take. All beings move toward pleasure and away from pain. As babies, we crawl towards the bright red toy and away from the too-bright light or the harsh sounds. As we develop further, we move from "me" to "us," and a desire to please others as well as to be pleased, to touch as well as to be touched. We begin to learn words for our emotions: anger, joy, disappointment, and excitement.

In our development as spiritual human beings, the sacral chakra's task, the heart of sensual and emotional pleasure, is to move us from the basic grounding of Earth, towards what we desire. It draws energy upward from our root chakra and expands from the material and physical towards the spiritual. The sacral chakra also helps us to balance the masculine, active principle, with the feminine, receptive and nurturing principle that exists within each of us.

Pre-Writing Meditations & Activities

Each day, before responding to the writing prompts, choose one of the following three meditation activities. Read each meditation through before starting.

Sacral Chakra Meditation #1

For this meditation, it may be helpful to play quiet music that reminds you of water — flute or piano — or sit near a fountain or other gently running water.

Sit or stand in a comfortable position. As with the root chakra, be sure your feet are flat on the floor. Place your right hand over your lower abdomen, with your little finger just above your pelvis. Then, place your left hand over the top of your right hand, with the thumbs touching.

Begin the meditation, in the same way as the previous lesson, breathing and sending golden roots deep into the Earth from your root chakra and the soles of your feet.

Draw the energy upward from the Earth into the root chakra. Pause here, imagining the spinning red ball. Send it love. As you breathe in, draw the energy upward into the sacral chakra where a ball of orange light pulses beneath the palms of your hands.

As before, notice how the light looks and feels. Is it a bright yellowish orange or a reddish orange? Is it spinning or moving in some other way? If so, which direction? Can you feel the energy? Just notice what you notice, without judgement.

If the ball seems sluggish, is not spinning clockwise, or wobbles, send it loving energy from the palms of your hands. Imagine this energy, like a finger of light, reaching out and spinning the ball faster and faster, until it spins on its own. Imagine the orange light glowing brighter and expanding until it fills your entire abdomen.

Now, move your consciousness down into the ball. Allow yourself to bask in the warmth of it, like lying in the sun on a warm day. Feel the sacral energy.

What do you feel?

When you are ready, let the orange light rise along the length of your spine, up through your heart, throat, forehead, and through the top of your head, connecting your entire body. Stay here for a few moments.

Where you are ready, let the energy return, little by little with each exhale, to its original source. Allow the ball to return to normal size, still spinning. Gently, withdraw your roots from the Earth and back into your body.

Sit quietly for a few breaths. When you are ready, open your eyes.

Sacral Chakra Meditation # 2

As with Sacral Meditation #1, it may be helpful to play quiet music that reminds you of water — flute or piano — or sit near a fountain or other gently running water.

Sit or stand in a comfortable position with your feet flat on the floor. Place your right hand over your lower abdomen, with your little finger just above your pelvis. Then place your left hand over the top of your right hand, with the thumbs touching.

Begin the meditation, in the same way as the previous lesson, breathing and sending golden roots deep into the Earth from your root chakra and the soles of your feet.

Draw the energy upward from the Earth into the root chakra. Pause here, imagining the spinning red ball. Send it love. Now, breathing in, draw the energy upward into the sacral chakra, where a ball of orange light pulses beneath the palms of your hands.

Imagine the ball of orange light expanding until it encompasses your whole body is encompassed in a luminous orange glow.

As the light suffuses your body, repeat the following affirmations:

On the exhale — *I release all negativity about my wants and desires.* On the inhale — *I receive with joy everything I desire.*

On the exhale — *I release all negativity and guilt about my sexual nature. On the inhale — I embrace my sexuality in its fullness.*

On the exhale — *I release all negativity and guilt I hold about receiving pleasure. On the inhale — I receive with joy and gratitude the sensual pleasures of my body.*

On the exhale — *I release all seriousness and tension from my body. On the inhale — I receive with gratitude a renewed sense of play and fun.*

On the exhale — *My creative energy flows easily from me into the world. On the inhale — I embrace my creative energy in all its fullness.*

Sit quietly for a few moments. Notice how you feel.

Moving Sacral Chakra Activity/Meditation #3

You'll need as much space as possible for this exercise. Wear comfortable clothing that allows you to move freely.

Select a piece of gentle, flowing, yet melodic music to play in the background.

Stand with your feet about shoulder width apart, back straight, hands at your side.

Close your eyes and pay attention to your breath for a few moments. As you breathe, imagine a spinning ball of orange light, just above your pubic bone, in the sacral area.

Imagine the energy of the music floating through the air and flowing into the orange ball, filling it and causing it to expand.

Let the light expand to fill your entire body and let the music move you. (Open your eyes for this part!).

Move in any way that is comfortable for you. Feel the air on your skin, the brush of your clothing, your heart beating, and the blood coursing through your veins. Be fully aware of the sensations of your body as you move and stretch, bend and sway.

When the music ends, stand still for a few moments. Notice the sensations in your body and how you are breathing.

Allow the light to return to the orange ball in the center of your sacrum.

Again, notice how you feel.

Writing Prompts

Choose one of the following prompts. Then, write for at least ten minutes in response to the prompt. Let your thoughts and feelings flow. If a particular incident or memory comes up, write about it. Get as much onto the page in ten minutes as you can.

When the ten minutes is up, stop, close your eyes and breathe, counting five long breaths. How do you feel? Open your eyes. If you want to write more, go ahead and write.

1. What did you experience during your sacral chakra meditation? What did you feel? What

memories or thoughts came to mind? Did you receive any insights about yourself or your life?

2. When you were a child, how were you taught to think about sexuality, and how has that affected you as an adult? Do you have a healthy, open attitude toward your own body and its physical desires, or are you uneasy with it? What feelings arise in you as you consider this topic? What colors are those emotions?

3. Do you have "control issues"? Do your friends tell you, or do you say of yourself, that you are a "control freak"? If yes, what are you afraid will happen if you don't control circumstances and events in your life? Write ten sentences beginning, "If I don't control _____ in my life I am afraid that..."

4. Are you experiencing any health issues or problems as described in the information section about the sacral chakra (low sex drive, reproductive problems, addictions to drugs or alcohol, depression or strong emotional swings, low back

pain, sciatica, urinary tract)? If so, what are they? How long have you had them? What emotional factors might contribute to these problems?

5. What is your relationship to wanting? Were you taught that it is wrong to want? Does wanting material things cause you to feel guilty? Or are you comfortable with material abundance?

6. What is easier, giving or receiving? Why?

7. Perform a word-association exercise with the word "sensuality." First, write the word *sensuality* at the top of a fresh page in your journal. Then, write the next word that pops into your mind. It's okay to repeat words — the key is to write continuously. List words without pausing until no more words come to you. When you are done writing, review the list of words and write a paragraph or two about what you notice.

8. Do you more often feel powerful or powerless? Write about a time you felt powerful. What were the circumstances? Who else was there? What

happened and how did it turn out? How has that event changed you?

9. Write for ten minutes about "orange."

10. What kinds of relationships do you have in your life? Do you have many friends or few friends? What about romantic relationships? Is there a theme that runs through your relationships with others? Write everything that comes to mind about relationships.

11. What is your relationship to creativity? Does creative expression seem to flow from you, or do you wrestle with it? Pretend that creativity is a person. Describe how s/he looks (colors/shapes), tastes (flavors), sounds, feels (emotional/physical), and smells.

Chapter Four

Taking Action
The Solar Plexus
Chakra

Manipura

Element: Fire
Color: Yellow
Sound: RAM

The solar plexus chakra, located between the navel and the lower chest, is our center of power. From the root chakra (Earth) and learning to ground and connect with Earth's energy, to the sacral chakra (water) and learning to flow with emotion, we now move to the solar plexus chakra, our fire center. The solar plexus chakra relates to our will, energy, metabolism, and our personal power (choice and autonomy).

Earth and water both flow downward; it is here, in this third chakra center, where fire ignites and moves our energy upward toward the higher chakras. Our solar plexus chakra gives us the energy and motivation we need to move upward toward the mental, intellectual, and the divine. One way to think about how this chakra functions is that it coordinates the energies of the lower two chakras and moves them upward, allowing us to use our conscious will to break out of the habits, emotions, and instincts of the unconscious.

This third chakra is our center of will and of choice. It is here that we commit to moving forward and making changes in our lives, transforming feeling to self-expression and desire to action. It is here that we form opinions and make decisions.

There are two kinds of power: power *over* someone or something — which is how we usually think about power — and power *with* someone or something. When we consider the power of the third chakra, it is this second type of power, a healing and uniting power. When we balance and heal our solar plexus chakra, we are reclaiming our personal power.

Will is purpose in action, which stems from conscious intent. That intent directs us to make certain decisions. It is both necessary and important to understand what purpose our will power is serving. What higher purpose or intent have we chosen? Once we understand this, then we can focus our decisions become more purposeful.

When healthy and open, the solar plexus chakra gives us unlimited possibilities to create, work, become what and who we want to be, and to move our lives in any direction. We feel confident. As we work with this chakra, we move toward autonomy, peace, and happiness with ourselves and the world.

When not healthy and open, we may experience digestive and/or metabolic disorders, hyperactivity or lethargy, low self-esteem, and a sense of failure. Or we might overcompensate and take on too many challenges, feel we have to prove ourselves to others, or that we have to gain power over others to feel good about ourselves. We may be driven by a need for success, for power, be Type A personalities, workaholics, unable to rest. Other symptoms of an unbalanced solar plexus chakra include needing to control others and intense stubbornness.

Or, life may feel like one big "have to." You may resent the circumstances of your life and say things like, "I *have* to work, I *have* to clean the kitchen, I *have* to live here, though I'd rather be somewhere else ..."

The truth is that we are always at choice. We can help heal our third chakra by reclaiming that sense of choice. Instead of saying, "I *have* to work," we can

say "I *choose* to work because I want to pay my bills."
We can say, "I *choose* to live in this town because it's
where I am." By moving our frame of reference from
"I have to" to "I choose," we begin to reclaim our autonomy and personal power.

In terms of our development and growth, this chakra is about individuation, where we separate from
our source, our authorities, and become individuals.
It's about having the courage and power to free one-
self from peer pressure (or any kind of coercive
pressure) and take decisive action for ourselves.

The initial development phase of our third chakra
occurs at about eighteen months, or soon thereafter.
This is the period of life parents like to call "the ter-
rible two's," because the child's own will wants to
assert itself over the will of the parents. The child
becomes aware that she has a self. "I want," becomes
a common refrain. The child makes connections between cause and effect and sees herself as separate
from her parents. She begins to develop a definition
of self.

Of course, a two-year-old is too immature to make decisions for herself, and parents often have to override her actions. This leads to conflict. If handled well — if sometimes she wins and sometimes she loses — this conflict can help her to develop a healthy sense of personal power. If handled poorly — for example, if she's completely dominated by her parents and is not allowed to make any personal decisions — she's going to withdraw, and her third chakra growth will be stunted. (If physical, emotional, or sexual abuse is involved, there needs to be healing in the root and sacral chakras, before healing and reclaiming of personal power in the third chakra.)

When we have not individuated, when our third chakra is not functioning properly, we have a sense of helplessness and lack of choice. Then, the natural tendency is to blame others for all the things in our lives with which we are unhappy.

When our third chakra is functioning, we have a strong sense of autonomy and purpose. We are centered in ourselves and in our bodies. And we also have a strong sense of personal responsibility and choice.

Pre-Writing Meditations & Activities

Each day, before responding to the writing prompts, do one of the following meditations or activities. Read each meditation or exercise through before starting.

Solar Plexus Chakra Meditation # 1

Sit in a comfortable position, with your hands cupped, right over left, thumbs touching and palms facing upward (not towards your body), over your solar plexus area. Your elbows will be out to the side.

As with previous meditations, send roots into the Earth and draw the energy upward into your root chakra. Pause here briefly, feeling the energy grounding and centering you.

Send the root chakra love and draw the energy upward, to the sacral chakra. Pause here, imagining a bright orange ball of light. Feel the fluidity of your emotions.

Draw the energy upward one more time, to the solar plexus chakra, beneath your cupped hands. Feel the power of this energy. Visualize a bright yellow light, the sun of your chakra system, burning brightly, and spinning clockwise.

Say, "I am power."

Now, as you breathe in imagine energy coming down from above, through the crown of your head, traveling down through your upper chakras and meeting the flame of the solar plexus chakra.

Say, "I am power."

Imagine the energy continuing to flow, from both directions, into and feeding the fire of your solar plexus chakra.

Repeat the mantra, "I am power," feeling the energy expand and fill your body.

Affirm: "I am powerful. I can be everything I want to be. I choose the direction of my life. I am in control of myself and my responses to anything that happens to me. My solar plexus chakra is clear and strong. I accept responsibility for myself. I am powerful."

Stay in this place for a few minutes, feeling the powerful energy in your body.

Allow the energy to merge back into the bright yellow ball of your chakra.

Gradually, open your eyes and withdraw your roots, imagining the bright lights of your first, second, and third chakras continuing to spin without your help.

Solar Plexus Meditation # 2

Sit in a comfortable position, close your eyes, and follow your breath in and out of your body for a few minutes. Feel tension flow out of your body with each breath, and energy flowing in.

Imagine the energy flowing in to your solar plexus chakra, feeding the flames of the yellow glow within you.

Continue to breathe naturally, noticing what you see (visualize) and what you feel, for at least 10 minutes.

Turn your attention back to your breath in the normal manner, noticing it flowing in and out of your body.

Open your eyes.

Solar Plexus Meditation #3 (calming)

For this meditation, lie down on a firm surface, such as the floor, on your back with arms to the side, palms facing upward (the "corpse pose" in yoga).

Close your eyes and imagine a brilliant yellow flower, petals open, floating just above your solar plexus.

With each breath, imagine the flower floating upward with each inhalation and downward with each exhalation, coming to rest again just above your solar plexus.

Do this for 5 to 8 minutes.

Writing Prompts

Choose one of the following prompts. Then, write for at least ten minutes in response to the prompt. Let your thoughts and feelings flow. If a particular incident or memory floats to the surface, write about it. Get as much onto the page in ten minutes as you can.

When the ten minutes is up, stop, close your eyes and breathe, counting five long breaths. How you feel? Open your eyes. If you want to write more, go ahead and write.

1. Write about your experience of your sacral chakra meditation or activity. What did you experience or feel? What memories or thoughts came to mind? Did you receive any insights?

2. Think about when you were a young child, the way that power was handled in your family and how you responded to it. Who held the power? Was it your father, mother, brother, sister, you? What was the means they used to exert their power (threaten, manipulate, withdraw, proactive, assertive, etc.) and how did you react to it (comply, rebel, withdraw, manipulate)? Write about what it was like to be you in your family.

3. (Do #2 before doing this prompt). Now, as an adult, when you are in a situation that involves the same power dynamics as in your family of origin, how do you respond? What do you do? Do you still act the way you did when you were a child? Is that response/reaction still serving you in a positive way, or is it something you'd like to change?

4. Do you feel that your life has purpose? If so, what is the higher purpose that drives your decisions?

5. Write about something in your life that feels like a "have to." Describe it and then describe what

you'd rather do. Write all the reasons you have to do that thing. Now rewrite what you've written above. In each place you wrote "have to" write the words "choose to" What does the result look like and feel like?

6. Write about a time where you rebelled against a rule, a dictate of someone else, or a situation in your life. What did you do to claim your power in that situation?

7. Draw something using shades of yellow. Write about what you drew and how you felt after your completed your drawing. What are you going to do with your drawing?

8. Notice, choose, and act: Notice if there is something in or about your life you don't like. What would you choose to have or do differently? What is a first step you could take to initiate that change?

Chapter Five

Balancing Mind, Body, and Heart
The Heart Chakra

Anahata

Element: Air
Color: Green
Sound: YAM

The heart chakra is at the center of your body over the sternum (not over the left side of the body, the organ of the heart). The heart chakra involves the whole chest cavity, the heart and lungs, the breath, and even the arms and hands. Breath — air — is the expansive element of this chakra.

The symbol for the heart chakra is two intersecting triangles. The bottom one, reaching from the Earth below upwards to spirit, and the upper one pointing down from spirit to Earth. At the exact center of this intersection is the heart chakra, the center of the entire chakra system, the fourth of seven.

The heart chakra represents perfect balance between the physical and the ethereal, male and female, earth and sky. It is the vibrant green of life and of healing. It is where we integrate and balance after we have sent our roots deep into the earth, learned to flow with our emotions, and taken control of our lives.

The energy of the heart chakra is love, the most talked about force in the world. "All you need is love..." But the love of the heart chakra differs from the emotion of the second chakra, which is about need and physical attraction. The heart chakra love is compassionate, an unconditional love and sense of wellbeing that radiates through you and outward to others. It is about the relationship of you to everything else in the universe, and it allows you to have and experience compassion for all living beings. It is without borders and without limits. This kind of love can be considered "divine" love.

It is here, in our heart chakra, that we want to learn to come into balance with ourselves: mind/body, work/rest, masculine/feminine, self/other. Once we find this balance, we have a stable platform from which to live life and build relationships. We don't have to struggle to maintain ourselves and can reach out to others easily.

The heart chakra engages and integrates the energies of all our chakras. When we are solidly rooted through our base (root chakra), are in touch with and allow the free flowing of emotions (sacral chakra), centered in our power (solar plexus chakra), can communicate our truth (throat chakra), and share vision and spirituality (third-eye and crown chakras), we have a better chance of having balance in our relationships.

Before we can achieve balance in relationships with others, we need to achieve balance in our relationship with Self. We must be able to experience total acceptance and unconditional love toward the first person with whom we have a relationship — the person in the mirror. This doesn't mean we are perfect, and it doesn't infer that we need not develop and grow and change. Achieving balance in our relationship with Self means we allow the energy of self-reflection, which is a place of the heart, to focus our will and purpose. This acceptance is the starting place for personal growth and development.

The heart chakra is where we look inward, reflecting upon ourselves (Why did I do that? What is my motive?). Focusing on the heart chakra helps us take a loving, accepting, yet discriminating look at ourselves to decide what needs to expand and what needs to contract to achieve balance.

Our heart chakra begins its developmental phase when we, as children, become conscious of our need for love and begin shaping our own personalities. Because we desire approval we change our behavior, repressing behaviors, such as tantrums, to win approval and love from our parents and other important people in our lives. We also begin to display some altruistic interests or behaviors, as well as shape our personalities to draw more love to us.

We notice relationships with others. We develop our social persona, learn to cooperate with other children at preschool, develop gender identities, and play-act roles. This social persona is not our true self, but a way of getting along in the world and receiving as much love as possible. As we grow older, we can make the mistake of believing this persona to be who we are, but it is a made-up being, an illusion of self.

To receive love, we reject parts of ourselves that we perceive to be unacceptable to others. Boys deny their feminine side and girls deny their masculine side. We learn that it's not acceptable to cry, or to show anger, or weakness. In this way, we become divided within ourselves.

As adults, working on the heart chakra means understanding and reclaiming those parts of us we rejected as children. One way to understand what aspects of Self you've rejected is to look at your relationships with others. Think about the irritating or unacceptable traits of people in your life — these are aspects of yourself that you have rejected. Learning to accept and love these shadow traits of self will help to bring you back into balance.

When you are balanced, you can express unconditional love, empathy, and sympathy, without losing yourself. You will not get involved in damaging relationships; instead, you will experience balanced, satisfying and intimate relationships. It's not that you'll become judgmental; you will simply make more appropriate relationship choices.

You'll be able to express love in a way that is open and free, allowing space for the people you love to develop and live their lives in their own ways. Balanced relationships allow healthy space, give and take, and result from two individually balanced people meeting and interacting in the center.

When your heart chakra is balanced, you'll have a strong immune system. Conversely, when you feel emotional pain, it is easier to get ill; this results from a weakened immune system.

One way that the heart chakra can be injured is through our relationships with parents and other family members. The tragedy of abuse is that it's often done in the name of love. Hitting, sexual abuse, over protectiveness and smothering, may all be perpetrated by parents who think they are showing the child love. Children love their parents no matter what they do and equate the abusive behavior with love, often repeating that same behavior when they become parents.

Grief through loss, whether through separation, divorce, death, or other types of loss can imbalance the heart chakra energies.

Damage to the heart chakra can cause emotional withdrawal from the world, coldness, a tendency to be critical, low self-esteem (affecting the solar plexus chakra), and a tendency to be manipulated in intimate relationships. You might feel pessimistic, suffer depression and feel a great sense of isolation, fear of relationships, and lack of empathy for others.

The reverse of withdrawal is to become so focused on receiving love that you engage in codependent behaviors. You might think you're sacrificing or giving up yourself for someone else, when the hidden purpose of your behaviors is to fill your own needs. You might become demanding and possessive, requiring someone else to be there for you all the time. This is not love. It's neediness and doesn't reflect a balanced heart chakra.

Most of the time, a blocked heart chakra is about not accepting and loving the self. We can't reach out to others until we have learned to love ourselves, and most of us don't know how to do this.

Only when we take responsibility for filling our own heart chakra, for loving ourselves, and for bringing balance to our own center, can we enjoy balanced, full relationships with others.

Pre-Writing Meditations & Activities

Each day, before responding to the writing prompts, do one of the following meditations or activities. Read each meditation or exercise through before starting.

Heart Chakra Meditation # 1

Sit in a comfortable position. Put a hand over your sternum and listen/feel for your heartbeat as you breathe.

Gaze at the intersecting triangles of the heart chakra symbol below. As you do so, feel the current of energy rising from the Earth, anchoring your root chakra. Feel it rising through your sacral chakra, flowing upward and into your solar plexus chakra.

Feel the power of will centered there. Then feel the energy continue upward to your heart chakra.

Keeping that picture in mind, feel the energy flowing downward, through your crown, through your head and neck and into the heart. Imagine the two energies intersecting and mingling in perfect balance one with the other.

Imagine this energy filling your heart chakra with vibrant green light — the result of all the light spectrums meeting in the middle — growing and filling your body, expanding to fill the room, expanding further to include your neighborhood and, then, the world.

Feel unconditional love, acceptance, and peace flooding you and extending to the world around you.

When you are ready, gently and slowly allow the light to return to your body and your heart chakra. Hold onto the feeling you experienced from the merging energies as you end your meditation and open your eyes.

Heart Chakra Meditation # 2

This is a simple meditation that can you can do in only a few minutes. Or, you can stay in it for long periods of time. The longer you perform this meditation, the more expansive and open you will feel.

Sit in a comfortable position, breathing normally. Notice your breath as it enters and leaves your body.

Open your arms wide. With your next breath, imagine drawing love energy from all around you into your heart. As you do so, bring your arms in, drawing that energy with your hands, to your heart.

As you exhale, open your arms wide, sending love energy out through your heart chakra and into the world.

Continue to breathe deeply and evenly, drawing love energy to yourself with your arms and hands, and releasing it outward with your arms.

When you are ready, let your arms fall to your sides and breathe normally for a few minutes. Notice how you feel.

Meditation to Release Grief

Make sure you are in a safe and undisturbed place for this meditation. Find a comfortable position, either lying or sitting. If you have them, hold a rose quartz crystal (resonates with love) and a picture or photograph of the person or object you are grieving.

Breathe quietly, listening to your heartbeat. Feel loving energy flowing into your heart chakra, upward from the Earth and downward from the universe through your crown.

Think about the person or thing you have lost and allow yourself to feel anything that comes up. Be gentle with yourself. Allow yourself to express tears and sounds. Remember to keep breathing. If you notice you are holding your breath, start again by taking a deep cleansing breath in and out.

Imagine healing, loving energy expanding from your heart chakra and surrounding the person or object, bathing him, her or it in that healing light.

Stay here as long as you wish, sending love to this person or thing.

Now, with a deep breath, allow yourself to let go. Imagine this person or thing rising upward, bathed in this loving energy, and floating away. As the person or thing floats away, imagine the bonds that held you together gently separating.

Now, hold your hands over your heart and imagine energy coming in to your body surrounding your heart and healing it with a comforting light. Stay here as long as you like.

When ready, open your eyes.

Writing Prompts

Choose one of the following prompts. Then, write for a minimum of ten minutes in response to the prompt. Let your thoughts and feelings flow. If a particular incident or memory comes up, write about it. Get as much onto the page in ten minutes as you can.

When the ten minutes is up, stop, close your eyes and breathe, counting five long breaths. How do you feel? Open your eyes. If you want to write more, go ahead and write.

1. Write about your experience of your heart chakra meditation or activity. What did you notice? Any insights?

2. Think about your family of origin. How was love defined and expressed in your family? What kinds of behaviors make you feel loved? How do you know when someone cares about you? How do you show others you care? What about your own children? Is the way you show love similar to the way your parents showed their love to you, or is it different? What other questions come up for you?

3. Write a letter about yourself as if you were your best friend, or another person in your life who loves and admires you. Write, as that person, why s/he loves you so much. List all your admirable traits and all your foibles that are

endearing. When you have finished writing the letter, read it to your reflection in a mirror. How do you feel afterward?

4. Make a list of all the traits you can think of in others that drive you crazy: perpetual lateness to events; talking too much, withdrawing when angry; self-absorption; overly critical; whatever. Make the list as long as you can. Keep writing until no more words come to you. Then, looking into a mirror, read the list to yourself, with "You are..." before each word "and I love and accept you the way you are" after each word. For example, "You are self-absorbed and I love and accept you the way you are." "You are overly critical and I love and accept you the way you are." Etc. How do you feel?

5. What does the word "compassion" mean to you? When you experience compassion from others, what is it like? How is it expressed and how does it feel? When you feel compassion towards others, how do you express that compassion? What

prevents you and what helps you to be a compassionate person?

6. Think about what it means to be balanced. Describe what it would look and feel like in your life.

Speaking Out
The Throat Chakra

Vishuddha

Element: Ether (space)
Color: Blue
Sound: HAM

Having traveled upward from our basic instincts for survival and sense of place, through our sexuality and emotional center, having created a sense of self and claimed our own power, and having channeled these energies through unconditional love, we give voice to who we are through the Throat Chakra. This chakra is the center of communication, creativity, integrity, and expression. It is the bridge between the intellectual/spiritual self and the feeling self. It allows us, finally, to share what we feel, what we think, and what we dream.

The throat chakra is about all forms of communication, including speech, writing, singing, chanting, and non-verbal communication, such as dancing and art. It relates to listening, knowledge of self, and the expression of all knowledge. It helps us to know our inner truth and convey it to the world.

Physically, the fifth chakra governs the thyroid, jaw, neck, mouth, ears, throat, tongue, larynx, shoulders, and shares the arms and hands with the heart chakra.

When you have low or blocked energy in the throat chakra, you may experience neck and shoulder problems, jaw disorders (such as TMJ), throat problems (chronic sore throat or laryngitis), thyroid problems, general issues communicating with others, or creative blocks. You may have a fear of speaking in groups or in public. Your voice might be shrill or high and pinched sounding.

When you have too much energy in the throat chakra, you may have problems listening to or hearing others, talk too much, and/or experience thyroid problems.

When you have a healthy, balanced chakra your voice will be strong and confident. You are a good listener, able to communicate clearly, live life creatively, and feel in integrity with yourself.

To a great extent, it's important to have healed our lower chakras in order to bring our fifth chakra into balance. The chakras each affect one another. For example, you can't be in your power without speaking up, and you can't speak up unless you claim your power. You will not be able to express your feelings, unless you have learned to experience your feelings and allow their flow through your energy centers. If your lower chakras are blocked, it is likely that you will also have problems expressing your truth.

When we have the support of the lower chakras, our creative energy bubbles up and into our fifth chakra, emerging in full expression. Our consciousness, coming down through the upper chakras informs that creativity and becomes a conscious act of art.

You may not think of yourself as a creative person, but everyone is creative. That is our nature as human beings. As you go through your day, everything you do is a creative act — how you wash the dishes, set the table, make the bed, or clean the house has creative and unique components to it. (Think cleaning the house is not creative? Think Martha Stewart.) Doing things a little differently and consciously from time to time will enhance your creative expression.

Truth telling is extremely important to our integrity as human beings, yet when we are young, we learn to lie in small ways. Our parents make us hug Aunt Lily, even though we think she smells bad. We learn to be polite: "If you can't say something good, say nothing at all." And we learn to suppress our truth, yet this habit of holding back imbalances the vibration of our entire being.

The throat chakra begins to develop during a child's years of exploration, approximately ages seven to twelve. This is when we have established a social identity and are moving on to a time of imaginative activity, play, and creativity. We begin to experiment. If you were not allowed to speak your truth, you would have had to narrow or shut down your throat chakra. But the truth wants to come out, and we have to shut down the whole body in order to suppress it.

Parents can help children discover their own truths and their creativity by encouraging them to play and to explore their interests. On the other hand, by discouraging creative exploration, parents may contribute to damaging or slowing the development of the fifth chakra.

The way communication occurs in your family also has an effect on your throat chakra's development. Think about how communication occurred in your family. What was it like? If you felt that no one listened to you, after a while you may have shut down. You may have stopped hearing your own inner voice. If you were lied to a lot, you probably grew up mistrusting all communication. If there was a lot of violent communication, yelling and screaming, you may have disassociated in an attempt to shut down your ears.

Truth is unique for each of us. It includes, not only how we respond to the world around us, but also our dreams, hopes, and desires. When we are able to clearly speak our truth, we are then in resonance and full integrity with our inner, physical, and auric bodies. Other people can hear and respond to us, because what we express resonates as genuine.

Our truth also changes. What was true for us last month may not be true now, and it is important to be tuned in and be able to express that change of opinion or sense of self. Doing so will help us also to be more compassionate with others. We understand that we each have a unique and personal perspective on the world and on life. We can listen to others' truths without feeling threatened, because we are confident in the knowledge of our own. We are also better able to accept where we (and others) are in our personal growth and evolution through life.

The throat chakra challenges us to be courageous and responsible, to be willing to stand up and say what we know to be the truth, and to keep our truth alive and present as we change our minds and perspectives.

This chakra also helps us define what we really want in life. It helps us to find our vocation, our life's work. And, like our truth, this can change as we grow and develop as spiritual human beings.

A fully developed throat chakra provides the gifts of clairaudience, channeling, and telepathy. Clairaudience is inner hearing — that voice in your head that tells you to turn right when you were going to turn left. Later, you discover that by turning right you avoided being involved in an accident. When you learn to hear and follow this voice, you feel more in tune with your intuitive connection to the universe.

Channeling allows us to communicate with higher spiritual beings (or at least to your inner higher being), to channel information and wisdom to this world in a language we can understand. Many gifted writers have stated that when they are writing, they feel they are simply channeling information, or that the stories seem to write themselves. You may have heard of some of the more famous channeled beings: Abraham, Seth, and Orin.

Telepathy is similar to channeling, but is more about tuning in to other people on this spiritual plane. Examples of telepathy include that sudden "knowing" that something is wrong with a loved one who lives on the other side of the U.S., or knowing what your lover is thinking or about to say. This gift allows us to send messages as well as receive them — sending out love and forgiveness, for example. Most of us have had the experience of thinking about someone and then having that person call us a day or two later, though we might not have heard from him for years.

Chanting, singing, speaking, and reading aloud all help to activate and open the throat chakra. Sound is essentially vibration and every vibration has rhythm that resonates with the cells of our bodies. To demonstrate to yourself, put your hand on your throat and chant *HAM* (pronounced "hahm") a couple of times. You will be able to feel the vibration of the sound in your throat and in your hand. When we chant, the vibrations affect our auric bodies, as well as our physical bodies. Singing and chanting can help bring us into resonance with all aspects of our being.

When we are in harmony with our own auric body, we can then know and speak our truths. We resonate with the universe as well as with ourselves.

Pre-Writing Meditations & Activities

Each day, before responding to the writing prompts, do one of the following meditations or activities. Read each meditation or exercise through before starting.

Throat Chakra Activity # 1

Sit in a comfortable position. Close your eyes and follow your breath for a few minutes, until you feel quiet within yourself.

Inhale deeply, then chant "HAM," feeling the vowel and the closing "m" to resonate in your throat, your ears, your body. Continue chanting for at least five minutes. (Alternatively, you can chant vowels or chant your name.)

Sit quietly. Notice how you feel. When you are ready, open your eyes.

Throat Chakra Activity # 2

Make sounds by playing with wind chimes, beating on a drum, sounding a crystal bowl, or playing a musical instrument. Do not try to structure the sound, but play with it; experiment with the different tones of the instrument.

Feel the vibration of the sounds as they enter your ears, are interpreted by your brain, and resonate throughout your body.

Do this for 5-10 minutes or more. Notice how you feel.

Throat Chakra Activity #3

This is similar to Activity #1, except when chanting, think about a chakra before you chant. For example, think about your solar plexus chakra. Allow your consciousness to settle there. Then, chant the sound for that chakra, or allow yourself to chant whatever note or sound feels right.

Continue chanting, experimenting with tone and vibration, while keeping your mind focused on the chakra you chose.

When you are finished, notice how your feel in the area of that chakra. Notice how you feel in the area of your throat chakra.

If you have time, do this exercise progressively. Beginning with the root chakra, focus on the chakra while chanting its sound. After a while, move upward to the sacral chakra, and so on, and complete the exercise with the throat chakra.

Throat Chakra Activity #4

This activity is helpful if you often talk too much or experience a lot of noise in your life. It can be challenging, but also extremely powerful.

Select a period of time, from two to eight hours, and commit to being in silence during that time. This means not talking, listening to music, writing, singing, taking in or expressing any form of communication.

You can perform activities, such as going for a walk, cleaning the house, etc. As you go about your activities be as present in your body and in your silence as possible.

At the end of your silent period, how do you feel? What kinds of thoughts did you have? Did you miss speaking? If so, how did that feel?

Writing Prompts

Choose one of the following prompts. Then, write for a minimum of ten minutes in response to the prompt. Let your thoughts and feelings flow. If a particular incident or memory comes up, write about it. Get as much onto the page in ten minutes as you can.

When the ten minutes is up, stop, close your eyes and breathe, counting five long breaths. How do you feel? Open your eyes. If you want to write more, go ahead and write.

1. Write about your meditation activity. What was it like? How did you feel at the beginning and then at the end? Did anything change?

2. Think about when you were a child, between the ages of seven and twelve. Were you supported in your creativity? Were you encouraged to take classes in or practice art, dance, or music? Were you given tools to explore your creativity? Was creativity valued in your household?

3. When you were a child, what was communication like in your family? Did people talk and work things out? Or did they become silent and withdrawn? Did everyone yell? Were you listened to or ignored? Were you encouraged or discouraged to speak your truth? Did you feel heard or did you feel that what you thought didn't matter? How do you think your home communication affected your throat chakra? How does it affect you now?

4. Create a dialog between your adult self and child self. What would your child self say about her truths? As the adult, really listen to the child. What is she saying that she was unable to say before? Listen more deeply. What were you always trying to say? Does any of it still hold true, or has it changed?

5. Think about your life now. Do you feel comfortable speaking your truth to those around you? If not, what holds you back? If yes, what allows for this expression? How have you made room for the expression of your truth in your life? If you've been holding back your truth, write what you've been holding back.

6. After reading this section about the throat chakra and doing some of the activities, are there any changes you'd like to make in your life that will enable you to more clearly speak your truth? If so, what are they, and how will you go about making the changes?

Chapter Seven

Receiving Inspiration
The Brow Chakra

A
j
n
a

Element: Light
Color: Indigo blue / purple
Sound: OM or AUM

From the throat chakra, the vibration of sound, we move upward into the vibration of light, traveling from sound to image. Words are symbols for communication. Images are even more efficient symbols for communication. (There is truth to the adage, "a picture is worth a thousand words.")

The third-Eye, or sixth, chakra is located in the forehead, the geometric center of the head, between the brows. It is also referred to as the brow chakra.

Its Hindu name, Ajna, means to know, to command, and to perceive. It is here, in the sixth chakra that we come to understand and take command of our lives. It's about seeing, inner vision, intuition, clairvoyance, and dreams.

Though all of our chakra work so far has helped us to move our lives forward and take control of them, it is here in the third-eye chakra that miracles and manifestations of desire are born. Some have called it the chakra of the sixth sense.

The awakening of the sixth chakra opens us to incredible gifts of magic — the kinds of things we believed in when we were young children, before people told us they didn't exist. As a child, you were probably imaginative and sensitive, but most modern cultures don't value these sensitivities. As a people, we are taught not to pay attention to dreams. We are not encouraged to be imaginative or to develop intuitive thinking. We are taught that what we can interpret through our five physical senses are the only measures of reality. And when, as children, adults contradict what we intuitively feel to be true, we become confused and begin to reject our intuitive perceptions.

The sixth chakra enables us both to see with our physical eyes and to see within ourselves. It offers a deep, inner vision. Seeing, even in the physical sense, is about more than just looking. It's about interpreting what we see, about taking the bits of data and recognizing patterns, and where they fit into the larger scheme of things.

For example, when you see an apple, your mind takes the data — shape, color, light and shadows — and recognizes the patterns, identifying it as an apple. You then place this into the larger scheme of your physical world. It is the same process with intuitive vision — a recognition of patterns and identification of where those objects fit in the larger scheme of the spiritual world.

As the light of consciousness shines through the window of our third-eye chakra, the images we create are passed through our other chakras on their journey to manifestation. When our chakras are open, the energy passes through and manifests our visions and dreams in the physical plane. However, if the lower chakras are not open and balanced, the pure image of our original vision can be distorted. Manifestation can be altered or blocked altogether by lies (fifth chakra), damaged relationships (fourth chakra), lack of will (third chakra), stored emotions (second chakra), and/or a lack of sense of place and right to receive (first chakra).

As our third-eye chakra opens, life seems to flow more easily. Things and events we've wished for seem to come to us without effort. The secret is being open to the flow of the spirit.

In all of our work so far, we've used the tools of the brow chakra — affirmations and visualization — to help clear, balance, and heal our chakras. Visualization is a powerful tool and is used around the world to improve physical performance (athletes often use it), in the treatment of illness, and in bringing positive results to every area of life. In recent years, the concept of creating our realities and manifesting our desires has become a trendy marketing tool, and we may be tempted to reject it as too centered on materialistic goals. Yet visualization is powerful in every context, and it is almost impossible to receive anything without it.

As an example of how simple and effective visualization is, I offer this anecdote. Some years ago, when I was teaching a dance class, many of the men were having trouble coordinating their steps with the beat. I paused the music. I then asked all the students to close their eyes and visualize performing the dance while I played the music and called out each step. I did this twice, taking about five minutes in total for the visualization. When I asked them to open their eyes, take their partners, and perform the dance in real time, *everyone* in the class performed the dance flawlessly. It was the first time I had used visualization this way, and the difference in performance astonished me.

Visualization is a natural ability. Thoughts appear in our minds first as images. These images then pass through our lower chakras on the path to manifestation. Therefore, it's important to know how we think about ourselves. What images are you passing through your chakras about yourself? Do you think of yourself as fat or thin? Successful or a failure? Happy or sad? All of these images (visualizations) of self affect how our desires manifest in the physical plane.

When we pull together the purest energies of our chakras — our vision, creative truth, loving heart, good intention and confidence — anything is possible.

The negative or dark side of the sixth chakra is illusion, which keeps us from seeing clearly. We see each other and ourselves through the filter of our illusions. On the extreme end is delusion — an anorexic thinking she is fat, a person suffering hallucinations or delusions of grandeur. These kinds of illusions drive us compulsively. True vision only *guides* us, and we are always free to make our own choices.

Through the sixth chakra also comes the gift of intuition. When this chakra is balanced, your intuition is active and you're able to hear it more easily. You'll be more perceptive and visually aware of what is going on around you. You'll experience a strong sense of imagination, be able to visualize, create new possibilities, and receive a guiding vision for your life.

Vision, intuition, and knowledge are all passive qualities. We can't force them. Instead, they flow to us and through us. Clearing and opening the third-eye chakra requires, in part, surrendering to the flow of spirit.

Dreaming is another aspect of the third-eye chakra. Dreams come from the realm of the unconscious and speak to us in symbolic ways. If you pay attention to your dreams, you will come to a better understanding of your inner sense of reality. Bringing dreams from unconscious symbols to conscious understanding can help resolve deeply held issues. For this reason, it's a good practice to write down dreams. Once you start writing them down, you'll remember them more fully. It's as if your subconscious knows that you're paying attention to it and tries to help out by becoming more available.

The sixth chakra controls the pituitary gland, the eyes, head, and lower brain. Physical symptoms of a blocked or unbalanced sixth chakra include headaches, eye problems, difficulty concentrating, forgetfulness, tumors, strokes, seizures, and blindness.

Emotional symptoms include passive aggressive behavior, preoccupation, excessive worrying, a feeling of disconnectedness with the body, and nightmares.

Therapies that work well to help open and balance the third-eye chakra include working with color (painting, water coloring, or other forms of art therapy, and surrounding yourself with the different colors of the chakras), reading, feeding images to the mind by going to art galleries, guided visualizations, and daydreaming.

Pre-Writing Meditations & Activities

Third-Eye Chakra Activity #1

Sit or lie in a comfortable position and close your eyes. Breathing normally, allow yourself to relax and feel the tension leave your body.

Imagine that you are sitting in front of a window. The window is fogged so you can't see through it, and is all white.

As you gaze at it, the fog fades, and you are able to see through the window to your ideal life. There is your ideal home in its ideal surroundings. You can see yourself performing your ideal work or daily activities with competence and joy.

Allow the visualization of your ideal life to unfold bit by bit, noticing the details. What are the colors? Is the sky blue? Are there birds? Pets? Children? Does your ideal life include a special relationship? What work are you doing?

If you want, you can focus on just one aspect of your ideal life.

How do you feel as you see this ideal life?

Stay with this visualization as long as you like. Before leaving, send gratitude and thanks to your chakra, affirming with confidence that you can have this ideal life.

Third-Eye Chakra Activity #2

This is a fun exercise to help strengthen awareness of your unconscious self, through symbols and images in your dreams.

Keep a dream journal for one week. (Put a notebook and pen or pencil on your nightstand, right next to the bed.)

In the morning, before you get up and before you reach for your notebook, review and rehearse your dream(s) in your mind. Re-visualize the images, colors and feelings in your dreams. This will make it easier to keep those images long enough to write about them.

Write everything you can remember about your dreams. Keep track of colors, numbers, the images themselves, and especially the feelings you had in the dream, such as fear, excitement, or confusion.

Once a day, preferably later in the day, review your dream journal entries and make note of recurring symbols, situations, and/or feelings. Ask yourself what the meaning of each symbol might be and, if an answer comes into your head, write it in the margins of the notebook.

Third-Eye Chakra Meditation

Sit or lie in a comfortable position. Breathe gently and allow yourself to let go of any stress or anxiety. Feel your body relax.

Bring your focus to your sixth chakra, to that place between your brows. See it glowing with a bright indigo blue light. Imagine the light cleansing and opening the chakra. Imagine it shifting colors to deeper blue perhaps, or purple.

Allow images to appear. They may fade and new ones appear. Or one image might become very detailed. Notice what images appear.

When you are ready, gradually allow the images to fade and open your eyes.

Writing Prompts

Choose one of the following prompts. Then, write for a minimum of ten minutes in response to the prompt. Let your thoughts and feelings flow. If a particular incident or memory comes up, write about it. Get as much onto the page in ten minutes as you can.

When the ten minutes is up, stop, close your eyes and breathe, counting five long breaths. How do you feel? Open your eyes. If you want to write more, go ahead and write.

1. Do Third-Eye Chakra Activity #1. When you have finished, describe the ideal life that you saw during your visualization with as much detail as possible.

2. Describe your experience with any of the activities or meditations. Focus on your feelings, insights, and thoughts during the process. What came up for you? Do you feel a direction for the future?

3. Describe your experience with intuition. When you were young, were you encouraged or discouraged to listen to your intuition? In relationships with others, did you distrust or trust your own sense of what you should be doing? Do you consider yourself to be a strongly intuitive person? Why or why not? What else about intuition comes to mind?

4. If you have had any experience(s) with clairvoyance, channeling, or prophetic visions, describe one or more of those experiences. When they occurred, what were you doing? How would you describe your spiritual state of being at the time?

5. What helps you to feel most connected and in touch with your inner, intuitive self?

6. Do you have vivid dreams that are easy to remember? Or do you struggle to remember them? Have you kept a dream diary? Was it helpful for you to understand your inner world? Does dream or symbol interpretation come easy to you, or does it leave you perplexed?

7. Write the word *vision* at the top of a page in your journal. Then write the next word that pops into your head (this is called free word association). Continue to do this writing every word down, without censoring, until no more words come to you and you feel quiet and empty. Then look at the words. Play with them, rearrange them. Do you see any patterns or themes? Finally, how was this process for you?

Chapter Eight

Mind and Spirit
The Crown Chakra

Sahasrara

Element: Thought
Color: white / gold
Sound: NG

We are approaching the other end of the rainbow bridge, from the red earth to the pure white light (golden or violet light, in some traditions) of consciousness.

The crown chakra is where consciousness (the soul), thought, universal truth, knowledge and understanding enters. From here, through the realm of thought and consciousness, we can transform the physical and connect with the divine. We can become liberated from the limitations of humanity and tap into divine Knowledge and Truth (yes, with a capital K and T). It is, indeed, the center of connection to consciousness and spirituality, and integration of body, mind, and spirit.

Consciousness itself is a mystery. It has no limits, is beyond space and time, and is unknowable in its entirety. We may ask ourselves, "Who is it that reads these words? Who is it that lives in this body and experiences this life? What does it mean to be me?"

To meditate on our own awareness is to explore the infinite. When we open to consciousness through the crown chakra, we open to a vastness in which we are but a small part. You could say that it is a way of opening to the heavens, and it would be true. Yet it is not only outward, but also inward, giving truth to the saying, "as above, so below."

Awareness of Self is awareness of the inner being, or witness — that awake, perceptive part of us that is unattached to our thoughts and experiences, and only observes. The witness is without judgment. It reflects us back to ourselves and is therefore a source of wisdom and knowledge. It is the inner voice that calls attention to our state of being, that part of us that seems to look down as if from afar, allowing an objective perspective.

It is in our seventh chakra that we look for and create meaning about what we experience in our daily lives. We build meaning upon meaning to create a worldview, developing belief systems around these life experiences.

In order to grow mentally and spiritually, it's important to continuously question our own thinking processes and not become too attached to meanings or beliefs that result in a limited worldview. One way of breaking out of a limited view of the world is, when we think we know the meaning of a particular situation, to try to find several other possible explanations. This encourages us to think from a broader perspective and helps to develop a more expansive worldview.

The negative side of the quest for meaning is attachment. We have to have some attachments, such as attachments to our children and our family, to goals (at least long enough to accomplish them), and to commitments. Attachment to life itself helps us survive — it's our anchor to the world. But when we become fixated on something — whether it be physical or intangible, such as a belief or thought, or someone — we are limiting our ability to connect with the divine and to "know the unknowable."

Letting go of attachments allows us to open to the universe and gives us access to knowledge and truth. This access is like riding an elevator to the top of the tallest building in a city. From the roof of this building, you have a broader perspective and a better understanding of the activities in the city, and you are less likely to get caught up in any one thing. You can see the traffic accident on the corner, as well as how it happened, without getting stuck in the resulting traffic.

Through the crown chakra, we receive wisdom and information from this broader perspective, which is then sent or channeled through the other chakras. When we transform our human limitations, we're not leaving behind or abandoning our lower chakras, but including them in the transcendent experience.

When the crown chakra is closed or blocked, you may experience depression, unhealthy attachments, be close-minded in your thinking and unwilling to question your thoughts or beliefs. You may be fixed on the only one, "true" way and feel alienated and alone. Physical symptoms include diseases of the muscular and skeletal systems, the skin, chronic exhaustion, as well as an over-sensitivity to light, sound, and environment.

When the crown chakra is open, you have a strong spiritual connection, and a healthy, curious, and intelligent mind. You are open-minded, can think for yourself, receive guidance from others, and are able to question your own beliefs, as well as the things you were taught.

When the crown is too open or is out of balance, you may be overly focused on intellectual pursuits or experience addictions to spiritual practices and dissociation from the body. In this case, it's important to bring your consciousness to the lower chakras and ground your energy in the Earth.

In terms of bringing the crown chakra into balance, there is probably no better practice than meditation. It calms us emotionally, clears our minds, and allows us to meet our internal witness.

Pre-Writing Meditations & Activities

Crown Chakra Meditation #1

Find a place where you will not be disturbed. Sit or stand in a comfortable position.

Pay attention to your breath. Breathe slowly and evenly, conscious of the flow of air in and out of your body. With each exhale, feel the tension flowing outward from your body. Allow yourself to fully relax.

Picture all your chakras, in a line from your root to your crown, completely open and spinning happily.

See energy rising from the Earth and flowing upward through your root chakra, to and through your crown chakra, as a white light. See it extend up above your body, continuing into the heavens, beyond the sky into space, beyond into the galaxy, and beyond, as far as you can imagine.

At the same time, imagine energy flowing downward through that beautiful column of white light, channeling through your open chakras, and into the Earth beneath you.

Feel the delicious openness of your chakras and of your body, as the energy simultaneously fills you and flows through you.

Stay here as long as you want. When you are ready, release your consciousness from the visualization and open your eyes.

Notice how you feel.

Crown Chakra Meditation #2

Sit or lie in a comfortable position. Breathe slowly and deeply, feeling the tension leave your body with each breath.

When you feel completely relaxed, imagine a bright beam of white light, of conscious energy, coming down from the universe and through the top of your head.

Imagine it filling the top of your crown with white light, then moving to the brow chakra. As it passes through the brow chakra, the light becomes a brilliant indigo blue.

The light continues to pass downward. As it passes through the throat chakra, it becomes a bright sky blue.

As it passes through the heart chakra, an emerald light expands and fills your heart area, your chest, your arms and hands.

As it passes through the solar plexus, the color shifts to sunlight yellow, radiating warmth and confidence.

The light continues downward, through the sacral chakra, where it glows orange, and finally, into the root chakra, a beautiful, rich red.

As the energy continues downward it shifts again to white and continues into the Earth, centering and rooting your energy.

You are now filled with light, all the colors of the chakra. You are a being of brilliant light.

Stay with this visualization as long as you want.

Crown Chakra Meditation #3

Sit or lie in a comfortable position.

Pay attention to your breath. Breathe slowly and evenly, conscious of the flow of air in and out of your body. With each exhale, feel the tension flowing out from your body. Allow yourself to sink into the Earth, fully relaxed.

Imagine a glowing ball of brilliant white light hovering just above your crown. Imagine this light represents divine consciousness.

Imagine it growing until it illuminates your crown. Let it continue to expand until your entire body is illuminated with white light.

If you have any questions, ask the white light, and wait for the answer(s). Allow yourself to be bathed and cleansed with the white light. Notice how you feel.

Now imagine the light gradually fading to invisibility. The light is not gone, only invisible. Notice again how you feel.

When you are ready, open your eyes.

Writing Prompts

Choose one of the following prompts. Then, write for a minimum of ten minutes in response to the prompt. Let your thoughts and feelings flow. If a particular incident or memory comes up, write about it. Get as much onto the page in ten minutes as you can.

When the ten minutes is up, stop, close your eyes and breathe, counting five long breaths. How do you feel? Open your eyes. If you want to write more, go ahead and write.

1. After doing any of the meditations, free write about the process. How did you feel during the meditation and how do you feel now? What did you think about? What was your experience?

2. For the most part and as a general rule, do you usually feel more isolated and alone, or connected? Can you easily access your higher self, or is it a struggle? Write about your experience.

3. When you are most connected to divine consciousness, what do you feel is your purpose in life? Do you have a strong sense of a calling? If so, what is it? If not, what do you think and feel about that?

4. Do you often experience awareness of your inner witness? Do you remember the first time? How would you describe that experience?

5. In your own words, define what the term *awakening* means to you.

Chapter Nine

Integration
Healing & Balancing

We have studied and meditated on the seven chakras as individual centers of energy, each related to a different aspect of our being. However, it's important to remember that at all times, all of our chakras are functioning in one way or another. For example, when you are working, you are engaging your mind on a conceptual level, visualizing results, and communicating with others. You are in relationship with coworkers, vendors, clients and bosses. You make decisions, process sensory information and feelings, and do what you need to do to survive on a daily basis.

Depending on what you are doing at any moment, some chakras are more engaged than others. If you are painting or writing, for example, you are engaging your fifth and sixth chakras, the centers of visualization and creativity, while your sacral chakra may be humming quietly in the background.

While reading, meditating, and writing about each chakra, you may have identified imbalances in one or more. While focusing on healing and balancing individual chakras is a good idea, it's also beneficial to get a sense of the state of overall balance of your chakra system — the balance of all the chakras in relationship to one another.

You can self-assess your overall balance by simply focusing on each chakra, one at a time, and then drawing what you see or sense in your mind about each chakra in relationship to the others. Begin with your root chakra. Is it large or small? Does it spin fast or slow? Does it seem weak in energy or have too much energy? Is it "just right?" Draw what you see. Continue this process, drawing each chakra, one above the other.

When you are finished, look at your drawing with an eye to the overall balance. When working to balance your chakra system, imagine moving excess energy from your stronger chakras to the weaker ones.

For example, if you see that your upper chakras — throat, brow, and crown — are vibrant and large, while the lower chakras — root and sacral — seem small and dull in comparison, then you need to move energy into your body from your mind and spirit. Ways to do this include adding physical activities to your life, meditating on the lower chakras, and sending energy from the upper chakras to the lower.

Many ways to heal and balance the chakras have been developed over the centuries. The meditations, exercises and prompts in this book can be helpful. I've also provided some additional references in Appendix A.

If things seem really out of balance to you, or it's apparent that some areas need a lot of healing, don't worry about it. Remember that you have all the knowledge and intuition within yourself needed to heal yourself. It's a matter of time, awareness, and attention.

Healing and integrating the chakra energies with awareness and intent is a wonderful journey that requires patience with and compassion for yourself. Enjoy the journey.

Manifestation

We have, during this book, moved from the lower to the upper chakras using a simplified, one-dimensional viewpoint from the front of the body. Each of the seven chakras operates through our bodies, front to back.

Energy flows in both directions, upward and downward, through our chakras.

Manifestation of thought to physical reality occurs via the downward flow of energy. A thought is conceived in the crown. As the energy of this thought moves downward, into the third-eye chakra, you receive inspiration. You develop a picture of this thing or event taking place in the world. As the energy continues to flow downward, into the throat chakra, the center of creativity and voice, you communicate about this thought, concept, or desire. The visualization or picture develops more fully. You might write about it, paint it, sing it, talk about it with experts.

In the heart chakra, your idea is put into relationships with others in your life. How will this desire to move out to the country affect your family or your coworkers? You give and take ideas, thoughts, feelings from others, filtering that feedback through your relationships.

When the energy moves into the solar plexus chakra, you're moved to action. This chakra gives you the ability, the power, to act on the idea. As you do this, pieces of your idea begin to manifest or occur. You begin to experience the physical aspects of what was originally a thought, moving the energy through the sacral chakra, the center for senses and emotions.

Finally, as the energy moves through your root, it becomes real and takes its place on this Earth. It becomes manifest. In this way, concepts become reality, thoughts become things.

When the chakras are not fully open and functioning, desires may be misplaced, energies get blocked, and you may see only limited or partial manifestations of your thoughts.

When the chakras are open and fully functioning, the manifestation process will occur with ease. Things will seem to just fall in place for you, as you receive inspiration and spiritual guidance. You'll feel that you are flowing along with the true current of life, experience great vitality, and a sense of joy and purpose.

Integration & Journaling Activities

Integration and Journaling Activity #1

Do the self-assessment activity as described in this section on integration. Start by drawing, on a large sheet of paper, an outline representing your body.

Within this body outline, make seven points that correspond to the placement of the seven chakras.

Then, one at a time, starting at the root, feel, visualize, and assess each chakra. Draw what you see/sense/feel about that chakra. Make notes around the outside of it if you wish. Continue this process upward through the crown chakra.

When you are done look at the whole picture. If there's an imbalance, are you imbalanced in one direction, with more energy in the upper or lower chakras? Are you imbalanced with more energy in the middle chakras and less in the upper and lower regions? Or vice versa?

Take ten minutes or more to write about what you see. As you write, tune in to the energy, wisdom, knowledge and truth flowing into you through your crown chakra, through the third-eye, throat, and so on. Do you receive any insights into ways to help balance your energies?

Integration and Journaling Activity #2

Put on some music and think about your chakras, visualizing each one and its connection and flow of energy to the next.

Begin moving with the music, slowly at first, and faster as you warm up.

Dance the movement of the energy beginning in the Earth, moving upward through the crown, and then back down again, finishing by grounding your energy in the Earth.

Sit or lie quietly for at least five minutes. Listen to your breath and your heartbeat. Feel the energy flow in your body. Notice how you feel.

Take ten minutes or more to write about this experience.

Resources

Books, & Recordings of Interest

(in alphabetical order by author's last name)

Chakra Balancing Kit (boxed set) by Judith Anodea (2006)

Eastern Body, Western Mind: Psychology and the Chakra System as a Path to the Self by Anodea Judith (2004)

Chakra Mantras: Liberate Your Spiritual Genius Through Chanting by Thomas Ashley Farrand (2006)

Hands of Light: A Guide to Healing Through the Human Energy Field by Barbara Brennan and Jos. A. Smith (Paperback — May 1, 1988), Bantam Books (1988)

Healing with the Chakra Energy System: Acupressure, Bodywork, and Reflexology for Total Health by John R. Cross and Robert Charman (2006)

The 7 Healing Chakras: Unlocking Your Body's Energy Centers by Brenda Davies (2000)

Color and Crystals: A Journey Through the Chakras (Crystals and New Age) by Joy Gardner (1988)

Vibrational Healing Through the Chakras: With Light, Color, Sound, Crystals, and Aromatherapy by Joy Gardner-Gordon (2006)

Vocal Toning the Chakras by Jonathan Goldman (2005)

Sounds of the Chakras by Harish Johari (2004)

Anatomy of the Spirit: The Seven Stages of Power and Healing by Caroline Myss (1997)

Chakra Breathing Meditations by Layne Redmond (2006)

Chakra Meditation: Discover Energy, Creativity, Focus, Love, Communication, Wisdom, and Spirit by Swami Saradananda (2008)

Chakras and Their Archetypes: Uniting Energy Awareness and Spiritual Growth by Ambika Wauters (1997)

The Book of Chakras: Discover the Hidden Forces Within You by Ambika Wauters (2002)

About the Author

Amber Lea Starfire is an author, editor, and creative writing teacher whose passion is helping others tell their stories. Her most recent books include *Not the Mother I Remember: A Memoir* — finalist for both the 2015 Next Generation Indie Book Awards and the 2013-2014 Sarton Women's Literary Awards — and *Week by Week: A Year's Worth of Journaling Prompts & Meditations*. Amber is also co-editor of the award-winning anthology, *Times They Were A-Changing: Women Remember the '60s & '70s*, and her creative nonfiction and poetry have appeared in numerous anthologies and literary journals.

Visit her online classes website and blog at writingthroughlife.com.

Other Books by Amber Lea Starfire

- *Not the Mother I Remember: A Memoir*

- *Week by Week: A Year's Worth of Journaling Prompts & Meditations*

- *Publish Your Chapbook! Six Weeks to Professional Publication*

Note from the Author

If you enjoyed this book, I hope you'll continue your journey of self-discovery by picking up your free guide, *10 Ways to Deepen Your Journaling Practice (https://writingthroughlife.leadpages.co/10-ways-to-deepen-your-journaling-practice/)* and by visiting writingthroughlife.com. There you'll find inspiration and resources to support every step of your writing journey, from journaling, memoir, and personal essay, to publishing.

I am also extremely grateful for your honest reviews and referrals. If you have time, please leave a review for this book on the site where you purchased it. Reviews help books to become more visible. And if you've told someone about *Journaling the Chakras*, thank you! Any way you can help spread the word is very much appreciated.

Made in the USA
Middletown, DE
28 January 2020